starting point

. . . .

A CONVERSATION ABOUT FAITH

Andy Stanley
and the Starting Point Team

REVISED EDITION

NORTH POINT RESOURCES

ZONDERVAN

Starting Point Conversation Guide Revised Edition
Copyright © 2014 by North Point Ministries, Inc.

This title is also available as a Zondervan ebook. Visit www.zondervan.com/ebooks.
Requests for information should be addressed to:
Zondervan, *3900 Sparks Dr. SE, Grand Rapids, Michigan 49546*

Photographs used by permission from Taylor Cox (taylorcox.tv), Mike Davis (redheadstepchild.com), Rick Holliday (rickholliday.com), Brian Manley (funwithrobots.com), Philip Sanders (threepennies.com), Jared Swafford (swingfromtherafters.com), John Ott.

The remaining images in this publication are licensed under the Creative Commons 0 License. Images are attributed to Adam Przewoski, Alejandro Escamilla, Amanda Sandlin, Chris Lui-Beers, Coley Christine Catalano, David Marcu, Dorothy Lin, Elisabetta Foco, Ilham Rahmansyah, Karin Margary, Linh Nguyen, Robin Rocker, Tom Butler, Victor Erixon, Vo Minh Thong, Wellington Sanipe, and Yoni Kaplan. The original versions of the images were retrieve from unsplash.com.

Cover photo by Taylor Cox; used by permission (taylorcox.tv).

Thirteenth Printing January 2018 / Printed in the United States of America

TABLE OF CONTENTS

WELCOME

Starting Point is a conversational environment where you can explore faith and experience community. It's a safe place for you to ask questions and to learn about the Bible and Christianity.

You may have questions that you've always wondered about but never felt you could ask at church, legitimate questions that would make many Christians uncomfortable. Ask them. Nothing is off-limits. We want to have conversations about the stuff that really matters to you, even when it's difficult to talk about—*especially when it's difficult to talk about.*

We believe that God loves you . . . specifically. And we believe he's big enough to handle your toughest questions, darkest moments, and deepest doubts. We want to honor him and you by creating an environment where you can be open, honest, and transparent.

Starting Point is designed for:

SEEKERS: those who are curious about God, Jesus, the Bible, or Christianity
STARTERS: those who have just begun a relationship with Jesus Christ
RETURNERS: those who have some church experience but have been away for a while

Whatever brought you to Starting Point, we're glad you're here. Enjoy the journey.

START

SECTION ONE:
A STARTING POINT

You had a first day of school, a first date, a first kiss, a first job. While many of our *first* experiences are the first in a series of similar experiences, some of our *firsts* are *starting points*. They represent the first points or steps on a journey. If you are married, that first date was more than a date, wasn't it? It was the starting point of a relationship. That first day of school was a starting point as well. Your career had a starting point. If you have children, your parenting had a starting point. But here's something you may not have considered—*faith has a starting point.*

If you grew up in a non-religious family, your first encounter with religious faith may have occurred at a neighbor's house or in school or it may be occurring right now. You may have been intrigued by the faith of others, or you may not have given it a second thought. Either way, you were aware that their experiences were different from yours.

If your faith began during childhood, you were probably taught some basic religious tenets: *God is good. God rewards good and punishes evil. God hears your prayers. God loves you.* These simple truths made sense in a world where the tooth fairy and Santa Claus made regular house calls. You may have had questions. Perhaps you even doubted at times. But the adults you trusted seemed confident in their faith, so you remained committed to yours—for the time being.

Fast-forward a few years and you found yourself confronted with adult realities for which childhood faith had not prepared you. You found yourself wrestling with questions such as: If God is *good* and *all-powerful*, why doesn't he do more to prevent the bad things in the world? Why does so much evil go unpunished? Why does prayer seem like such a shot in the dark? Why do bad things happen to good people? Why are some religious people so judgmental and mean? Why don't science and religion line up? Why does it seem that smart people are less religious?

Even as your faith shrank or your doubt solidified, you may have run into some "grownups" that had faith. Strong faith. Faith that didn't resemble a child's belief in the tooth fairy or Santa Claus. They maintained what looked to be an unshakable confidence in God in spite of what they saw or experienced. They didn't pretend to have all the answers. In fact, they didn't pretend at all. They were honest and hopeful. They acknowledged the complexities of the adult world, but their faith remained strong. Perhaps it was their faith that caused you to begin doubting your doubt.

If so, you are in the right place. That's exactly what this guided conversation is about. It's why we call these gatherings *Starting Point*. If you grew up without a faith framework or you've just begun a relationship with Jesus, this may be a *literal starting point* for you. If you lost faith along the way, you may see our time together as an opportunity to restart your faith. Regardless of where you are, we are honored that you have chosen to participate for the next eight weeks as we explore what it looks like to develop faith that doesn't merely survive the real world but thrives in it.

Ever since I was a little girl and could barely talk, the word "why" has lived and grown along with me . . . When I got older, I noticed that not all questions can be asked and that many whys can never be answered. As a result, I tried to work things out for myself by mulling over my own questions . . . So the word "why" not only taught me to ask, but also to think. And thinking has never hurt anyone. On the contrary, it does us all a world of good.

● Anne Frank

7

8

SECTION ONE:
QUESTIONS FOR REFLECTION

1 What did your faith look like growing up?

2 Would you say you are currently at a starting, turning, returning, or other point? Why?

....

....

....

....

....

....

....

....

....

....

....

....

....

....

....

Faith is trusting in advance what will only make sense in reverse.

● Philip Yancey

10

SECTION TWO:
ROOTS OF FAITH

Most Christians grow up being taught that regardless of the question, the answer begins with, "The Bible says." In childhood, this is enough. If God wrote a book, there is no reason to challenge what it says. But for some of us, "The Bible says" became problematic somewhere north of our eighteenth birthdays. Truth is, for faith to be unshakable, the foundation must be more substantial than a *book of miracles* written thousands of years ago. Right? A storybook may be enough to birth faith in a child. But a storybook is not enough to sustain faith in an adult. But if we dispense with the Bible, where do we go for our starting point? Where does faith begin?

All truths are easy to understand once they are discovered. The point is to discover them. That takes investigation.
● Galileo

The first Christians didn't use the Bible as a starting point for their faith. For the first two hundred-plus years of Christianity, Christians did not support their faith with a book. Their starting point was not something *written*; it was something that had *happened*.

As you probably know, the Bible is divided into two parts: the Old Testament and the New Testament. The New Testament contains the teachings of Jesus along with the narratives surrounding his birth, life, and crucifixion.

There are four accounts of Jesus' words and works. These ancient documents are referred to as the Gospels. While most agree that the Gospels were written during the years immediately following Jesus' life, they were not collected and published together until many years later. The term "New Testament" was first used around AD 250 in reference to one of the earliest collections of sacred Christian texts. Despite the fact that there was no Christian Bible, hundreds of thousands of men and women became followers of Jesus in the first three centuries. The starting point of their faith was not "The Bible says" or "The Bible teaches"; it was something else entirely. And we're convinced that something else serves as an adult starting point for faith in our generation as well.

The apostle Paul traveled around the Mediterranean planting churches in the first century. He found himself with some time to kill in Athens. He met a group of philosophers who gathered on a regular basis to examine new ideas. They were looking for a framework that made sense of the world. They knew more than most, but continued to pursue greater certainty by discussing the latest ideas. Like most people in their culture, they believed in a pantheon of gods. But they willingly acknowledged the gaps in their knowledge. They even erected an altar inscribed "To an unknown God." They were covering all their bases. If a new god arrived on the scene, they were ready for him. Or her. Or it.

Paul viewed this *just-in-case* altar as an opportunity to introduce his new friends to the central message of Christianity. He couldn't begin his presentation with "The Bible says" because there was no New Testament. In fact, at this point in history, none of the four Gospels had been written. So Paul drew their attention to the fact that curiosity regarding God was universal. He argued there was something in every man and woman that wonders, questions, and seeks. He went on to say that God actually wants to be found . . . so much so that he entered creation in the form of a man—*Jesus*. This God-man came to explain what God is like and to reconcile humanity to himself.[1]

This was not an easy message for Paul's skeptical audience to embrace. They had never heard of Jesus. The notion of a single god was difficult enough. The idea that this God had entered creation in the form of a man was outside the realm of possibility for most of Paul's Athenian audience. But one thing was certain. Paul was not asking them to believe a book. He never mentioned a book.

It's not that the Bible isn't important, but Paul was challenging them to put their faith in a person. The question he left them with is the question that anyone exploring faith must eventually answer. It is the question that serves as the starting point for the Christian faith. The question is, *Who is Jesus?*

The important thing is not to stop questioning. Curiosity has its own reason for existing. One cannot help but be in awe when he contemplates the mysteries of eternity, of life, and of the marvelous structure of reality. It is enough if one tries to merely comprehend a little of this mystery every day.

● Albert Einstein

---

1 Acts 17:16–34

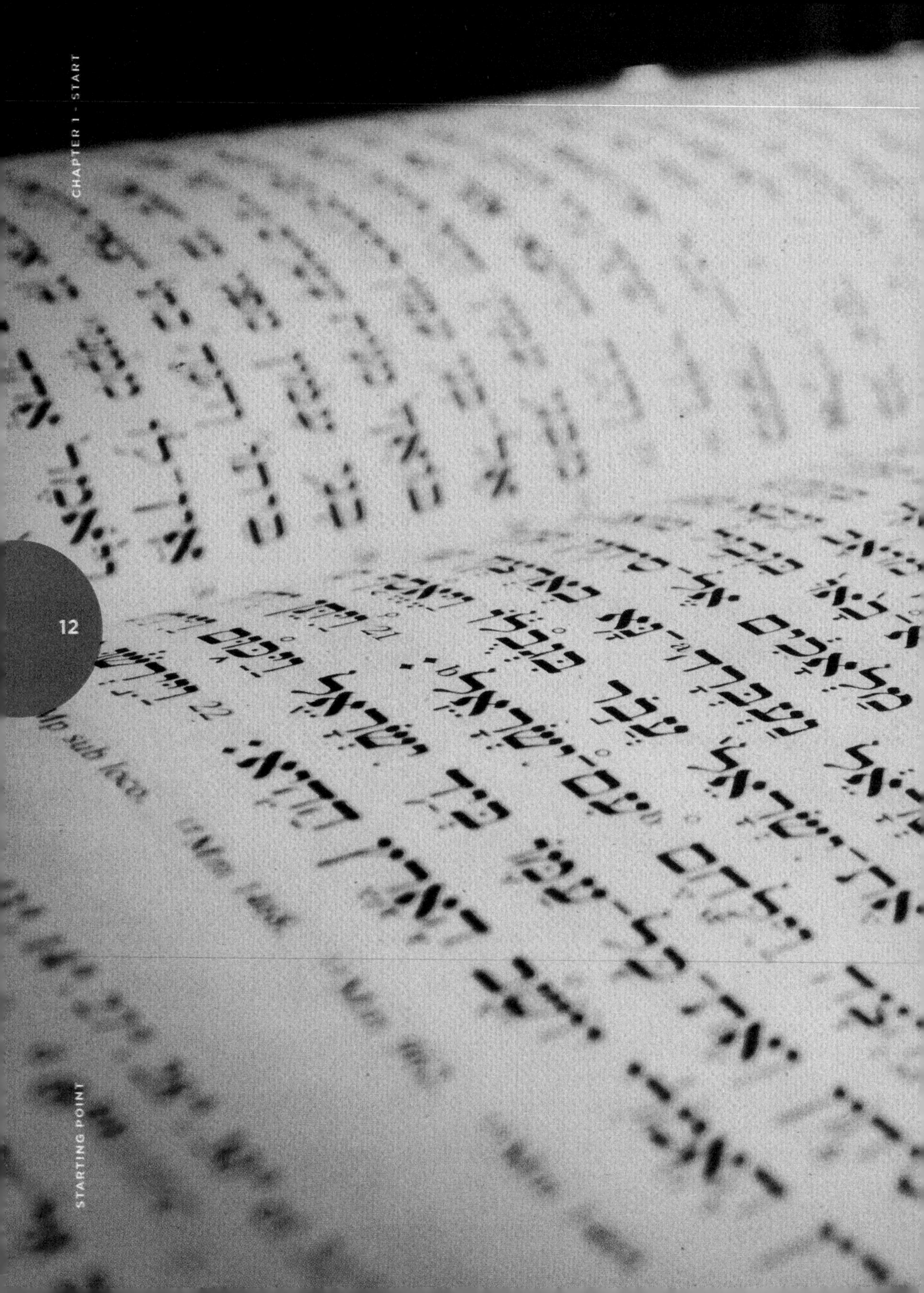

SECTION TWO:
QUESTIONS FOR REFLECTION

1 What do you associate with the Bible?

2 How has your view of God changed during different seasons of your life?

....

....

....

....

....

....

....

....

....

....

....

Most people are bothered by those passages of Scripture they do not understand, but the passages that bother me are those I do understand.

● Mark Twain

SECTION THREE:
WHO IS JESUS?

The name that was so new to the Athenians is one we have all heard today. Jesus is the central figure of the Christian faith. Interestingly, other faith traditions claim Jesus as one of their own as well. But Jesus' influence goes beyond religion. It is difficult to find anyone anywhere who does not respect Jesus. His teachings have shaped the consciences of nations. This Jewish carpenter, who never traveled more than a hundred miles from his birthplace, never wrote a book, never raised an army, and was a public figure for less than four years before being crucified by Rome, remains the subject of endless conversations, debates, books, movies, and controversies.

Who is he? What makes his life and teachings so unique? What sets him apart? Why do millions of people from cultures all over the world continue to follow him?

It's true that Jesus' teachings represented a radical departure from the established norms of his day. His version of generosity and compassion went head-to-head with the commonly held assumption that it was a waste of time to do anything good for someone who didn't have the means to return the favor.

He insisted that his followers pray and give privately while other religious leaders made a great to-do of praying and giving to be seen. While conventional wisdom said to love your friends and hate your enemies, Jesus taught his followers to love their enemies and to look for opportunities to serve them.

But it wasn't what Jesus said that ensured his teachings would survive the first century. It wasn't his insight, his parables, or even the events surrounding his death that catapulted his fame and renown into the next generation and the generations to follow. In fact, Paul didn't even mention Jesus' teachings to the Athenians. The reason men and women like the apostle Paul risked and eventually sacrificed their lives for Jesus was not what he said before he died but what happened afterward. Three days afterward, to be specific.

Jesus rose from the dead.

A religion that is small enough for our understanding would not be big enough for our needs.

💬 Corrie ten Boom

15

16

SECTION THREE:
QUESTIONS FOR REFLECTION

1 What do you hope to get out of your Starting Point experience?

2 What one question do you hope to have answered by the end of our eight weeks together?

17

....

....

....

....

....

....

....

....

....

....

....

....

....

....

....

....

At the end of the day, the questions we ask of ourselves determine the type of people that we will become.

● Leo Babauta

BOTTOM LINES FOR CHAPTER 1

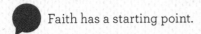 Faith has a starting point.

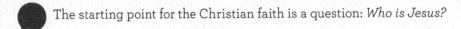 The starting point for the Christian faith is a question: *Who is Jesus?*

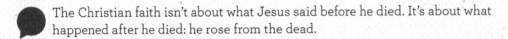 The Christian faith isn't about what Jesus said before he died. It's about what happened after he died: he rose from the dead.

FOR THE NEXT GROUP MEETING:

Read and complete the questions for Chapter 2. Watch or listen to the Chapter 2 message at spmembers.com

At the next group meeting, we'll talk about why we so often feel separated from God. We all have a set of standards that we don't live up to on a consistent basis. We imagine that God's set of standards must be higher than ours. If we can't live up to our own, then we certainly can't live up to his. And when we fail to live up to God's standards, we assume he condemns us. Is that true?

 Take advantage of essential chapter resources at:
spmembers.com

Today is when everything that's going to happen from now on begins.

● Harvey Firestone, Jr.

PROBLEM

SECTION ONE:
IT'S A MISTAKE

Last week, we determined that the starting point for the Christian faith is a question: *Who is Jesus?* Traditionally, however, the starting point for the Christian faith is an accusation: "You're a sinner."

Big difference.

Sin is an uncomfortable word. It's so uncomfortable that we've pretty much abandoned it. When kids disobey, parents don't respond with, "You've sinned against me." When an employee is late with a report, managers don't respond with, "Have a seat. We need to talk about your sins." Even judges don't use that term.

But we know we aren't perfect. So in our efforts to address the tension between our inability to get it right every time and our disdain for being categorized as never getting it right, we've adopted a new term

that falls somewhere in the middle: *mistake*. We aren't sinners. But we aren't perfect. We make *mistakes*.

There is a problem with using the term *mistake* to describe all our less-than-perfect decisions and behaviors. The problem is that label doesn't adequately describe everything we call a mistake.

A mistake is an *error* in action, calculation, opinion, or judgment caused by poor reasoning, carelessness, or insufficient knowledge. Mistakes are *accidental*. A mistake is something a sixth grader makes on a math test. A mistake is something adults make when filing their income tax returns. A mistake is something we learn from so we don't do it again. However, we've expanded that definition to include just about everything.

But sin harms our relationship with God and our relationships with other people. It's so deeply ingrained in all of us, we can't stop sinning.

How about a celebrity when it's discovered that he's been involved in a multi-year affair? He almost always refers to those recurring rendezvous as *mistakes*. But does *mistake*

Your best teacher is your last mistake.
💬 Ralph Nader

really capture the magnitude and nature of an affair? Offended spouses say no. Offended spouses feel betrayed. They might even reach back for the old-fashioned term *sin* to describe what their partners did.

Then there's this. Sometimes we make *mistakes* on purpose. Don't we? Don't you? Sometimes we *plan* our mistakes. Think about that. You are guilty of premeditated *mistakes*! What do you call a *mistake* you make on purpose? What's the best term to describe a *mistake* you make on a recurring basis? What do you call a person who plans and carries out the same mistakes over and over? A serial *mistaker*? Last question. What term should we use for a premeditated *mistake* that hurts another person?

Perhaps we've made a *mistake* substituting the term *mistake* for all things less than perfect. Perhaps we need a new term. Or perhaps we should reach back and resurrect an old term. As uncomfortable and as old-school as the term *sin* may seem, there is a benefit to reintroducing the word into our vocabularies.

Experience enables you to recognize a mistake when you make it again.
● Franklin P. Jones

23

24

SECTION ONE:
QUESTIONS FOR REFLECTION

1 Where have you experienced or observed the inadequacy of labeling something a *mistake*?

2 What do you associate with the word *sin*?

3 How do you respond to the consequences of having done something wrong?

Every age has its massive moral blind spots. We might not see them, but our children will.

● Bono

SECTION TWO:
REPEAT OFFENDERS

You may resist being branded as a sinner. That's understandable. But the truth is, it's a brand no honest person can avoid. A sinner is anyone who knows the difference between right and wrong and chooses to do wrong. On purpose. Sound like someone you know?

Perhaps your resistance to being branded a sinner stems from its close association with divine condemnation, alienation, and separation. Listen to the average street preacher and you may conclude that not only does being a sinner condemn you to hell, but also that God is actually looking forward to sending you there!

Jesus had a very different response to those wearing the sinner brand. When you read the Gospels, you can't help noticing that he was attracted to sinners. Never once do we find him threatening them with hell. Not once. In fact, just the opposite is true. Jesus' response to sinners was an offer of restoration. As a result, people who were nothing like Jesus liked Jesus. And he liked 'em back. Self-righteous religious leaders who peddled graceless religion were the only ones Jesus consistently condemned. Jesus had little patience for religious people who considered themselves sinless. He knew better. He knew they knew better as well.

Jesus taught that sin separates us from God, but that God's willingness to forgive reconnects us. So it was important to Jesus that men and women faced and embraced their status as sinners so they would recognize their need for forgiveness. Mistakers don't ask for forgiveness. Mistakers don't need forgiveness. Mistakers just need opportunities to do better next time.

When Jesus talked about sin, he made it so all-inclusive that nobody could escape. He said things like, "You have heard that it was said, 'You shall not commit adultery.' But I tell you that anyone who looks at a woman lustfully has already committed adultery with her in his heart."[1] Ouch!

Jesus raised the standard so high that nobody made a passing grade. Then he turned right around and insisted that God was on an endless pursuit to restore his relationship with sinners. The transaction that made this possible was a personal admission of guilt and a request for forgiveness. So, while being branded a sinner is uncomfortable, Jesus taught that it is necessary. Sinners need forgiveness. Forgiveness is the means by which humanity is restored to a right relationship with the heavenly Father.

---

1 Matthew 5:27–28

The difficulty we have in accepting responsibility for our behavior lies in the desire to avoid the pain of the consequences of that behavior.

💬 M. Scott Peck

28

SECTION TWO:
QUESTIONS FOR REFLECTION

1 What does the fact that Jesus was attracted to sinners say about him?

2 What does it cost a person to acknowledge he or she is a sinner?

3 Do you resist the idea of being called a sinner? Why or why not?

But until a person can say deeply and honestly, "I am what I am today because of the choices I made yesterday," that person cannot say, "I choose otherwise."

Stephen R. Covey

SECTION THREE:
ONLY ONE PERSON

The Gospels record breathtaking events in which Jesus extended forgiveness and restoration to individuals who were considered beyond redemption. One involved a woman caught in adultery. This was not a one-time occurrence. This was not a mistake. It wasn't an accident. She knew better. Jewish law required that she be stoned. Jesus, who taught that the law was good and should be obeyed, invited those who assembled for the stoning to go ahead and commence the punishment . . . but with one interesting caveat.

> "Let any one of you who is without sin be the first to throw a stone at her." - John 8:7

Jesus didn't defend her. Jesus didn't dumb down her sin. Jesus didn't give her any wiggle room. No talk of her desperate plight or her difficult upbringing. She was guilty as charged and deserved to be punished. Again, he invited it. But no one moved. No one threw a stone. Eventually, the crowd dissipated. The oldest members of the mob were the first to leave. Before long, Jesus was alone with the frightened woman. It was only then that he addressed her directly.

"Woman, where are they? Has no one condemned you?"
"No one, sir," she said. - John 8:10–11

What he said next is, well, breathtaking.

> "Then neither do I condemn you," Jesus declared. "Go now and leave your life of sin." - John 8:11

Jesus, who called people to an impossible standard of behavior, declared this condemned woman uncondemned. This apparent contradiction reflects the essence of Jesus' message and ministry. He did not condone sin. He did not condemn sinners. He called sin, sin. But instead of insisting people get what the law said they had coming, he extended the very thing sinning people deserved least: forgiveness.

Another incident is even more amazing. This one takes place during Jesus' crucifixion. The gospel writer Luke tells us that Jesus was crucified between two criminals. According to Luke, one of the criminals crucified with Jesus hurled insults at him. The other criminal, however, came to Jesus' defense.

But the other criminal rebuked him. "Don't you fear God," he said, "since you are under the same sentence?"
- Luke 23:40

What came next was shocking.

"We are punished justly, for we are getting what our deeds deserve."
- Luke 23:41

That's quite a statement. The criminal's behavior was so heinous, he not only believed he deserved to die, he believed he deserved to be crucified—a horrible form of execution in which people often suffered for days before dying. Referring to Jesus, he continues,

"But this man has done nothing wrong." Then he said, "Jesus, remember me when you come into your kingdom." - Luke 23:41-42

There's no way, right? He has no opportunity to do "better." There's no way to know if he's sincere. He's desperate. He would say anything at this point. Wouldn't you? That's what makes this story . . . breathtaking.

Jesus answered him, "Truly I tell you, today you will be with me in paradise." - Luke 23:43

Just like that, he's forgiven.

He's restored.

He's in.

> If life were fair, we'd get treated the way we treat others, and if life were fair, we'd get paid exactly what we are worth. And in the end, we'd all get exactly what we deserve. So, son, maybe it's better if life isn't fair. Sometimes I'm thankful that life isn't fair.
> ● Mike Williams

32

SECTION THREE:
QUESTIONS FOR REFLECTION

1 On pages 30–31, what, stands out to you about Jesus' interactions with the woman or the criminal?

2 Do you think Jesus' response to the criminal next to him was fair? Why or why not?

....

....

....

....

....

....

....

....

....

....

....

....

....

....

All that we call human history—money, poverty, ambition, war, prostitution, classes, empires, slavery—is the long, terrible story of man trying to find something other than God which will make him happy.

● C. S. Lewis

BOTTOM LINES FOR CHAPTER 2

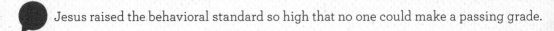

- Jesus raised the behavioral standard so high that no one could make a passing grade.

- God is on an endless pursuit to restore his relationship with sinners.

- Jesus never minimized the seriousness of sin, but he did not condemn sinners.

FOR THE NEXT GROUP MEETING:

Read and complete the questions for Chapter 3. Watch or listen to the Chapter 3 message at spmembers.com

During Starting Point, you'll have the opportunity to share your story with your group. Use the *What's Your Story?* section at the end of this guide to help organize your thoughts.

34

At the next group meeting, we'll talk about one of the most basic building blocks of faith. Most people assume that faith begins with obedience to God. We tend to imagine God as an authoritarian who demands we submit to him in exchange for his favor in our lives. But the Bible paints a very different picture of how God approached a relationship with humanity in order to begin to solve the problem of sin.

Take advantage of essential chapter resources at:
spmembers.com

For however devoted you are to (God), you may be sure that he is immeasurably more devoted to you.
Meister Eckhart

35

TRUST

SECTION ONE:
GOD'S DILEMMA

All religious or faith systems have histories, but most people are more interested in their personal faith experiences than they are in their personal faith's *history*. For example, most Christians know very little about the history of the early church. They can tell you what they don't like about their current church. But once you get beyond their personal church experiences, they don't have a lot to add to the conversation. That's true of most faith traditions. Religious people are generally more concerned with getting God to answer their prayers than they are with where the concept of a prayer-answering God came from originally. And that's unfortunate, because *faith based on personal experience alone eventually buckles under the weight of personal experience.* Perhaps that's your story.

Three major faith traditions share the same starting point. Consequently, there is a good bit of overlap in their views of how God views humanity. Judaism, Christianity, and Islam all agree that God created humanity in his image—the implication being there is something divine in each of us. All three religions agree that in the beginning God and man lived in harmony.

Another point of agreement is that God gave humanity the capacity to say yes and no to their Creator. Free will. These three ancient religions teach that early in the history of humanity, somebody said no. When that happened, sin entered the world and nothing since then has been as good as it was intended to be. The cost of sin is death. That's because humanity's relationship with God was broken. Sin ruptured the harmony. Sin has been rupturing harmony ever since.

The introduction of sin into the human experience left God with somewhat of a dilemma. It's probably not completely accurate to speak of God as having a dilemma. But best we can tell, he had a choice to make: *destroy this sin-infected world and start over, or roll up his sleeves and go to work fixing it.* Instead of walking away, he waded in. Where does one begin the task of restoring the world from the effects of sin? If you've ever knocked over a gallon of paint in your living room or dropped a two-quart glass container of salsa on your kitchen floor, you get the picture. You were probably tempted to move. But you didn't. You just picked a starting point and began cleaning.

God did the same thing. But instead of starting at a particular place, he started with a particular man. Judaism, Christianity, and Islam all agree that God began the cleanup process with Abraham.

Our God is an expert at dealing with chaos, with brokenness, with all the worst that we can imagine. God created order out of disorder, cosmos out of chaos, and God can do so always, can do so now— in our personal lives and in our lives as nations, globally.

💬 Desmond Tutu

40

SECTION ONE:
QUESTIONS FOR REFLECTION

1 Why do you believe what you believe? Consider people, circumstances, places, etc.

2 Have your personal experiences ever caused you to doubt or change your beliefs?

3 Why is sin so problematic for God?

Everybody experiences far more than he understands. Yet it is experience, rather than understanding, that influences behavior.

● Marshall McLuhan

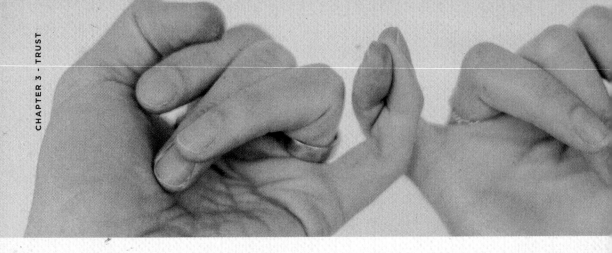

SECTION TWO:
GOD'S PROMISES

The story of Abraham begins around 1876 BC, long before Jesus or the prophet Muhammad, long before Moses and the Ten Commandments. Abraham was a man of wealth and influence. He had land, cattle, and servants. But there was one thing he didn't have: a son. In Abraham's culture, having a son—an heir—was a big deal. He would have traded everything he had for one son. That's why when God told him to pack up and leave the country in which he'd grown up, he did so.[1]

Abraham wasn't a perfect man. In fact, he was deeply flawed. Genesis records that he lied and cheated. Sometimes his faith in God was shaky. We'll never know why God chose Abraham as his first step in reconnecting with humanity. But we do know that God didn't wait for a perfect man to come along before he got started.

God's interaction with Abraham started with three promises.

> Promise 1
> "I will make you into a great nation." - Genesis 12:2

This came as a shock to Abraham. He was an old man at the time. His wife, Sarah, was beyond her childbearing years, and they had no children. God didn't simply promise Abraham a child. He promised that from him would come an entire nation! And that's exactly what happened. Israel, along with several Arab nations, claims Abraham as its father.

> Promise 2
> "and I will bless you; I will make your name great" - Genesis 12:2

Another way of saying that is, *I will make you well-known, famous.* That happened as well. Chances are you had heard of Abraham before signing up for Starting Point. How about Zoar? Heard of him? No? King Chedorlaomer? Don't feel bad. Their names all but disappeared a generation or two after

The best way to find out if you can trust somebody is to trust them.
💬 Ernest Hemingway

1 Genesis 12:1, 4

state funerals. But Abraham? Just about everybody has heard of the nomad Abraham.

The third promise God made to Abraham intersects with our modern era as well.

> Promise 3
> "and all peoples on earth will be blessed through you." - Genesis 12:3

Now that's a big promise. Not only would the world know Abraham's name, the world would be "blessed" through him. Literally, the world would be better off because of Abraham. It would have been one thing if God had promised that the people of Abraham's future nation would be blessed through him. But the promise was bigger than that. Much bigger. According to this promise, every people group on the planet would somehow be better off because of Abraham.

Every Jewish man, woman, and child who has ever lived is certainly better off because of Abraham. All people from the Arab nations that trace their lineages to Abraham would probably agree that they are better off. Muslims hold Abraham in high regard. Christians from every generation believe they are better off because of Abraham. Now consider the people groups who have been blessed directly or indirectly by the work, writings, discoveries, inventions, medical care, charity, and personal relationships with people from those groups. That's a lot of people. It may be everybody.

Trusting God completely means having faith that He knows what is best for your life. You expect Him to keep His promises, help you with problems, and do the impossible when necessary.

💬 Rick Warren

43

44

SECTION TWO:
QUESTIONS FOR REFLECTION

1 Do you think it was hard for Abraham to believe God's promises?
Why or why not?

2 What do you think of God choosing someone as imperfect as Abraham?

3 If you could hear one promise from God, what would you want it to be?

....

....

....

....

....

....

....

....

....

....

....

....

....

....

[I] know that love is ultimately the only answer to mankind's problems . . .

● Martin Luther King, Jr.

SECTION THREE:
COMING CLEAN

Even though God made Abraham three promises, Abraham didn't know how things would turn out. So, he did what we would do. He worried. Abraham and Sarah were still hoping for a son. Without a male heir, Abraham's chief servant, Eliezer, would inherit everything. The writer of Genesis tells us that one evening while Abraham was sharing these concerns with God, God spoke.

> Then the word of the LORD came to him: "This man will not be your heir, but a son who is your own flesh and blood will be your heir." He took him outside and said, "Look up at the sky and count the stars—if indeed you can count them." Then he said to him, "So shall your offspring be."
> - Genesis 15:4–5

As encouraging as that must have sounded, it didn't change the fact that Abraham and Sarah were old and childless. So Abraham had to decide whether to believe that God would keep this unbelievable promise. Abraham's belief dilemma set the stage for one of the most important statements found in the Scriptures. What followed was a declaration and clarification concerning

the starting point for humanity's relationship with God.

> Abram believed the LORD, and he credited it to him as righteousness.
> - Genesis 15:6

To state it another way, righteousness was credited to, or applied to, Abraham because he believed God's promise. If someone were to ask if you were righteous, chances are you would say no. We associate righteousness (or right standing with God) with good or perfect behavior. So how could righteousness be credited or applied to Abraham? That's an important question. Families have been divided and wars have been fought over that question. What does it mean that righteousness was credited to Abraham?

As the story of salvation continues to unfold through the Old and New Testaments,

God's promises are like the stars; the darker the night the brighter they shine.
● David Nicholas

the answer to that question becomes increasingly clear. Abraham was given the same rights and privileges with God that a perfectly righteous man would gain through his perfect acts of righteousness. Instead of earning a right standing with God through right actions, Abraham had it gifted to him in response to his faith. Long before the Ten Commandments were given to Moses, Abraham was given the label "righteous," not because of anything he had done—he was a sinner just like everyone else—but because he believed.

Two thousand years later, the apostle Paul would make a connection between Abraham's single act of faith and those seeking a right standing with God in his generation.

> This is why "it was credited to him [Abraham] as righteousness." The words "it was credited to him" were written not for him alone, but also for us, to whom God will credit righteousness—for us who believe in him who raised Jesus our Lord from the dead. - Romans 4:22-24

Paul's point? The righteousness available to Abraham is available to you as well. The means by which you attain a right standing with God is the same as well: faith. A single expression of faith.

If the notion of God granting something as important as righteousness on such simple terms is hard to believe, that's understandable. Relationally speaking, it's unprecedented. Maintaining a good standing with people requires that we behave a certain way. Other than our mommas, virtually no one extends that kind of unconditional acceptance. Is it possible that God would do such a thing?

When we contemplate the whole globe as one great dewdrop, striped and dotted with continents and islands, flying through space with other stars all singing and shining together as one, the whole universe appears as an infinite storm of beauty.

💬 John Muir

47

48

SECTION THREE:
QUESTIONS FOR REFLECTION

1 How do you know when someone really believes something?

2 What is the significance of Abraham being declared righteous?

3 What do you believe it takes for God to accept someone?

God loves each of us as if there were only one of us.

St. Augustine

BOTTOM LINES FOR CHAPTER 3

- The introduction of sin into the human experience left God with a choice. Instead of walking away, he waded into the mess.

- God's solution to the problem of sin began with three promises he made to one man.

- The righteousness available to Abraham through faith is also available to us.

FOR THE NEXT GROUP MEETING:

Read and complete the questions for Chapter 4. Watch or listen to the Chapter 4 message at spmembers.com

At the next group meeting, we'll discuss the role of rules in a relationship with God. We all have a love/hate relationship with rules. On the one hand, rules can provide structure and predictability. On the other hand, rules are restrictive and we all want to be free to do what we want, when we want. The problem with religious rules is that they usually run contrary to human nature. That makes them really hard to follow. And we assume that when we don't follow rules, God rejects us. But is that really true?

Take advantage of essential chapter resources at:
spmembers.com

In the middle of difficulty lies opportunity.
- Albert Einstein

RULES

SECTION ONE:

RELATIONSHIPS AND RULES

If you were raised in a religious home or attended a religious school, it was probably the rules that made you question whether religion had a place in your future. Perhaps the rules associated with the faith tradition you were raised in made you feel judged. A faith community may have even ostracized you. Truth is, most religious rules run contrary to human nature. And being the human that you are, that's a problem. Inconsistency in the way rules were applied and to whom they were applied may have left you with the impression that religion breeds hypocrisy. And, in fact, it does.

Religious people love loopholes. They look for loopholes in their faith systems to avoid the more restrictive rules. So, many Catholics have found ways to justify the use of birth control. Only a percentage of Muslims pray with their faces to the ground five times a day. Just a small number of Protestants show the type of kindness, love, and forgiveness that Jesus modeled. Religious people are generally better at *believing* than *behaving*. Every major faith tradition teaches some form of the Golden Rule: *Do unto others as you would have them do unto you.* But we're all guilty of excusing our way around that imperative. So, yes, religion seems to breed hypocrisy. At some level, we are all hypocrites.

In spite of that, all faith systems agree that in order to be in good standing, followers need to keep the rules. Belief and behavior are central in every major religion. Obedience determines whether you are a good Muslim, Christian, Sikh, or Jew. Whether it's the Five Pillars of Islam, the Ten Commandments of ancient Judaism, or Jesus' Sermon on the Mount, rules define proper and improper behavior within a faith system.

But here's something you may not have considered: *Rules always assume a relationship.* If you are a parent, you set rules for *your* kids. Imagine getting a call

Submission is not about authority and it is not obedience; it is all about relationships of love and respect.

● William Paul Young

from a neighbor checking to see if your kids are in bed. None of her business, right? She can't set rules for your kids. They are *your* kids. An individual's children are his or her children before the creation of rules. In fact, an individual's children are his or her children even if there aren't any rules. Relationship precedes the rules in a *family model*.

Family isn't the only model. In some cases, one's willingness to adopt or agree to a set of rules creates the relationship. In this scenario, the rules precede the relationship. Think of this as the *club model*. When you join a health club, hunting club, or country club, you have to sign a contract agreeing to abide by the rules. Agreeing to the rules is how the relationship is established. In this arrangement, breaking the rules can result in the termination of a relationship.

But which of the above models reflects the connection between rules and relationship in religion? Is it the *family model*, where disobeying the rules will get you punished but not necessarily kicked out? Or is it more like the *club model*, where you have to agree to the rules to get in and if you don't keep the rules, you're asked to leave? How you answer this question will determine the way you view God and the way you assume he views you.

Don't walk behind me; I may not lead. Don't walk in front of me; I may not follow. Just walk beside me and be my friend.

● Albert Camus

55

56

SECTION ONE:
QUESTIONS FOR REFLECTION

1 In general, how do you respond to rules? Do you tend to keep them or break them?

2 What were the most important rules for you growing up? Which rules are still important to you?

3 Which model, family or club, best represents your understanding or experience of rules and relationship in religion?

....

....

....

....

....

....

....

....

....

....

....

....

Good people do not need laws to tell them to act responsibly, while bad people will find a way around the laws.

● Plato

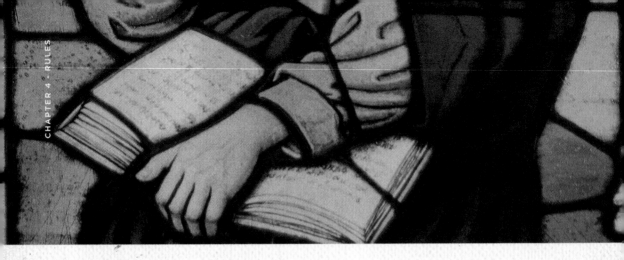

58

SECTION TWO:
GOD'S RULES

The Ten Commandments is arguably the most famous list of rules ever produced. Just about everyone in Western civilization is familiar with the Ten Commandments. But very few people can name them.

The Ten Commandments were given to ancient Israel about fifteen hundred years before Jesus was born and about twenty-one hundred years before the birth of Muhammad. The most significant thing about the Ten Commandments is not the commandments themselves. In many ways, they are quite ordinary. They prohibit adultery, murder, and theft. Nothing too surprising. What makes them important for our purposes is *to whom* they were given, *why* they were given, and *when* they were given.

In Chapter 3, we discussed how God promised Abraham that his descendants would become a nation and that the nation would bless the world. Eventually, Abraham and Sarah had a son, Isaac. Isaac had Jacob. Jacob had twelve sons, whose families became large tribes, who became known collectively as the Hebrew people. In order to escape a devastating famine, Jacob's sons and their families migrated to Egypt, where they lived for many years. Eventually, these Hebrews were enslaved by a Pharaoh. For four hundred years, the descendants of Abraham labored under the harsh and cruel treatment of Egyptian taskmasters. Then, around 1446 BC, Moses led what by this time had become the nation of Israel out of Egypt and back to the land of Abraham. It was during their journey back home that God gave Israel the rules.

The Ten Commandments are found in the Old Testament book of Exodus. If the term

We may not all break the Ten Commandments, but we are certainly all capable of it. Within us lurks the breaker of all laws, ready to spring out at the first real opportunity.
● Isadora Duncan

exodus reminds you of the English term *exit*, it should. This ancient document is the story of Israel's *exit* out of Egyptian slavery. About three months after they were delivered from their oppressors, the nation camped at the foot of Mount Sinai. Moses ascended the mountain and stayed there for over a month. When he returned, he brought with him God's law for Israel.

The sequence of events is important. It provides us with a valuable insight into the connection between God's rules *for* the nation and his relationship *with* the nation. Which came first, the relationship or the rules? Was one predicated on the other? If the answer to that question is not clear from the sequence of events, it is certainly clear based on what we find in the commandments themselves.

Most people are surprised to discover that the Ten Commandments do not begin with a command. Here's the opening line:

> And God spoke all these words: "I am the LORD your God." - Exodus 20:1-2

God declared his relationship with the nation before telling the nation what he required. God gave Israel rules because they belonged to him. He was their God and they were his people. The Ten Commandments were confirmation of, not a condition of, Israel's relationship with God. The second part of the statement underscores this:

> "I am the LORD your God, who brought you out of Egypt, out of the land of slavery." - Exodus 20:2

In other words, *I am the Lord your God who did something significant for you without*

requiring anything from you. Three months earlier, they were a nation with no hope and no future. Now they were free. And they had done nothing to deserve it. After defining and affirming their relationship, God issued his first command:

> "You shall have no other gods before me." - Exodus 20:3

After proving himself trustworthy to the nation, God asked the nation to trust him in return—to look to him as their ultimate authority and provider. God did not give Israel rules as a means by which to establish a relationship. From the very beginning, God adopted the *family model.* The people of Israel were his children. He was their Father.

SECTION TWO:
QUESTIONS FOR REFLECTION

1 What value do the Ten Commandments have today?

2 Have you considered that God declared a relationship with the people of Israel before giving the Ten Commandments? What do you think of this?

3 What rules do you think matter most to God?

Where there is no law, but every man does what is right in his own eyes, there is the least of real liberty.

Henry M. Robert

SECTION THREE:
YOUR ROLE

God loved Abraham. God loved Israel. But wouldn't it be presumptuous for you to assume God feels the same way about you? Relationship preceded rules with Abraham and Israel, but maybe God plays favorites. Perhaps for everyone else God opted for the *club model*—the "behave, or else" model.

God's ultimate purpose in choosing Abraham through which to create a nation was actually to bless the entire world. In fact, part of God's promise to Abraham was that the entire world would be blessed through him. Later, the prophet Isaiah would echo that idea when he wrote concerning Israel:

> "I will also make you a light for the Gentiles, that my salvation may reach to the ends of the earth."
> - Isaiah 49:6

God's plan, beginning with Abraham, always included all the nations of the earth. His plan included you! So, we should not be surprised to discover that when Jesus appeared fifteen hundred years later, he would extend God's offer of salvation beyond the borders of Israel. One of his closest followers, the apostle John, stated Jesus' intent this way:

Yet to all who did receive him, to those who believed in his name, he gave the right to become children of God. - John 1:12

Did you catch those last three words? "Children of God." Not "members of the club." Children.

An infinite God can give all of Himself to each of His children. He does not distribute Himself that each may have a part, but to each one He gives all of Himself as fully as if there were no others.

● A. W. Tozer

We need a new kind of relationship with the Father that drives out fear and mistrust and anxiety and guilt, that permits us to be hopeful and joyous, trusting and compassionate.

💬 Brennan Manning

64

SECTION THREE:
QUESTIONS FOR REFLECTION

1 Is there a connection between the way God accepted Abraham, accepted Israel, and accepts us? Explain.

2 Is it easier to see God as a rule maker or a parent with boundaries? Why?

3 What would change if you really saw yourself as a *child* of God?

....

....

....

....

....

....

....

....

....

....

....

....

....

God reveals himself to us not in a metaphysical formulation or a cosmic fireworks display but in the kind of stories that we use to tell our children who they are and how to grow up as human beings.

● Eugene Peterson

BOTTOM LINES FOR CHAPTER 4

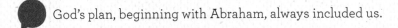

Rules always assume a relationship.

God's rules didn't establish his relationship with Israel; they were confirmation of his relationship with Israel.

God's plan, beginning with Abraham, always included us.

FOR THE NEXT GROUP MEETING:

Read and complete the questions for Chapter 5. Watch or listen to the Chapter 5 message at spmembers.com

Finding personal forgiveness for personal sin is often the starting point for personal faith. At the next group meeting, we'll talk about the role of personal forgiveness in a life of faith and Jesus' role in our learning to forgive others.

Take advantage of essential chapter resources at:
spmembers.com

It is after you have realized that there is a real Moral Law, and a Power behind the law, and that you have broken that law and put yourself wrong with that Power—it is after all this, and not a moment sooner, that Christianity begins to talk.

● C. S. Lewis

JESUS

SECTION ONE:
FINDING FORGIVENESS

If you're like most people, there's probably a chapter of your life you'd like to erase or go back and do over. It might have been as far back as high school or college. It may be a recent relationship. We've all made bad decisions we can look back and laugh about. But most of us carry memories that will never elicit anything but shame and regret. So, what do you do? You know what and whom you should avoid in the future. But what do you do about what you already did? Or what you are doing?

People often dumb down their dumb decisions by comparing them to other people's dumb decisions. Perhaps you've tried that. It certainly takes the edge off— *for a while.* Then there's the "Well, nobody's perfect" approach. And while that's true, it doesn't change anything. It certainly doesn't remove the shame or ease the guilt. Excuses and explanations are like aspirin. They provide temporary relief, but eventually the pain returns. Coping mechanisms help us cope. But coping mechanisms don't wash away the past. And at the end of the day, that's what we all need. Something that will wash away our mistakes—our sin.

Perhaps the previous two paragraphs surfaced memories you work hard to keep hidden in the recesses of your mind. So why dredge them up now? Here's why. Moving forward in your faith journey may require some looking back. While that may be uncomfortable, it could also be liberating. Addressing lingering shame and regret can lead to an experience that ignites personal faith in a way you may not believe possible. Experiencing personal forgiveness for personal sin is often the *starting point* for personal faith.

Guilt is perhaps the most painful companion of death.
● Coco Chanel

To forgive is to set a prisoner free and discover that the prisoner was you.

● Louis B. Smedes

72

SECTION ONE:
QUESTIONS FOR REFLECTION

1 What do you wish you could do over?

2 Do you resonate with the idea that you need to forgive yourself? Why or why not?

3 Do you believe you need forgiveness? Why or why not?

....

....

....

....

....

....

....

....

....

....

....

....

....

....

Accepting the reality of our sinfulness means accepting our authentic self.

● Brennan Manning

SECTION TWO:
THE MESSIAH

In the first century, John the Baptist showed up in the region of Judea preaching and baptizing. In addition to the Gospels, John the Baptist is referenced in the Quran as well as by the Jewish historian Josephus. John's message was harsh. Yet thousands flocked to the Jordan River to hear him.

Many believed John was the long-awaited Jewish Messiah. But he rejected that title. Instead, he claimed to be a forerunner of one whom God would send. His role was to prepare Israel for what was about to take place in their midst. He was the warm-up act, so to speak.

> "I baptize with water," John replied, "but among you stands one you do not know. He is the one who comes after me, the straps of whose sandals I am not worthy to untie."
> - John 1:26-27

One afternoon, while baptizing in the Jordan River, John looked up and saw Jesus standing in line, waiting his turn. John's response was staggering. Leveraging fifteen hundred years of sacred Jewish tradition, he declared,

> "Look, the Lamb of God who takes away the sin of the world!" - John 1:29

This statement is so packed with implication that it requires some detailed explanation.

When Moses came down from Mount Sinai with the law, the Israelites discovered that God included provision for sin. When an Israelite sinned, he was required to sacrifice an animal. The animal's blood covered, or atoned for, the sin committed. This was a bloody and poignant reminder of the cost of sin and the need for forgiveness. No one believed the blood of an animal was equal in value to the blood of a human being. But according to Jewish law, the blood of an animal was enough. The challenge was that sacrifices had to be done repeatedly. There was no final sacrifice for sin.

With that as a backdrop, consider the gravity of John's statement when he pointed at Jesus and said, "Look, the Lamb of God"—literally, the lamb God has provided for us. This Lamb, this man, would "take away" the sins of the world. According to John, through Jesus, sin would be lifted up and carried away once and for all. But not just Jewish sin. John was clear. Jesus would carry away the sins of the entire world. Jewish sin. Roman sin. Gentile sin. Your sin.

No one understood the significance of John's declaration that day. But toward the end of

Jesus' ministry, the truth of John's words came into sharp focus. Jesus had not come to take away the sins of the world in some symbolic fashion. He was *the* sacrificial Lamb of God who would literally take upon himself the sins of humanity. Through his voluntary death, he would lift up and carry away the sins of the world, once and for all.

On the night of his arrest, Jesus gathered with his apostles to celebrate Passover. During the meal, he said something that shocked and perhaps offended everyone in attendance. The Jews had celebrated the Passover meal for around fifteen hundred years. It traced its roots all the way back to the night before the Israelites left Egypt. God instructed the Israelites to take the blood of a lamb and place it on the doorframes of their homes. Death would *pass over* the homes marked by the blood of a lamb.

As Jesus broke bread and distributed wine to those gathered with him that night, he announced that from that night forward, when they gathered for Passover, they were to commemorate something other than their ancestors' departure from Egypt.

> And he took bread, gave thanks and broke it, and gave it to them, saying, "This is my body given for you; do this in remembrance of me." In the same way, after the supper he took the cup, saying, "This cup is the new covenant in my blood, which is poured out for you." - Luke 22:19–20

From that night forward, the Passover wine was to represent his blood, soon to be spilled on their behalf. The bread was to remind them of his body, which in a few short hours would be broken for them. Jesus was making an outrageous claim. He had already rattled

the status quo on several occasions when he claimed authority to forgive sin. Now he was claiming to be the sacrifice for sin.

The next day, as Jesus took his last breath while hanging on a cross, his followers believed they were witnessing a tragic and confusing end. But Jesus had predicted his own death as the necessary sacrifice for sin. His death was the final sacrifice of God's final "lamb."

If our greatest need had been information, God would have sent us an educator. If our greatest need had been technology, God would have sent us a scientist. If our greatest need had been money, God would have sent us an economist. But since our greatest need was forgiveness, God sent us a Savior.

💬 Roy Lessin

75

76

SECTION TWO:
QUESTIONS FOR REFLECTION

1 Why is the title "Lamb of God" significant?

2 According to the text, how is Jesus connected to our need for forgiveness?

3 Why was Jesus' death necessary?

Salvation was bought not by Jesus' fist, but by His nail-pierced hands; not by muscle, but by love; not by vengeance, but by forgiveness; not by force, but by sacrifice.

● A. W. Tozer

BE STILL AND KNOW THAT I AM GOD

SECTION THREE:
ONLY ONE PERSON

Christians believe Jesus was the Lamb of God who picked up and carried away the sin of the world. That's great news for you. Here's why. *You don't have to forgive yourself; yourself has already been forgiven.*

The sin you've tried to make up for, pay for, and find redemption for has already been made up for, paid for, and redeemed. It happened two thousand years ago when the Lamb of God took away the sin of the world—including your sin.

About twenty or so years after Jesus' crucifixion, the apostle Paul described the significance of that tragic, glorious event this way:

> He forgave us all our sins, having canceled the charge of our legal indebtedness, which stood against us and condemned us; he has taken it away, nailing it to the cross.
> - Colossians 2:13–14

Through Christ, God has "canceled" your sin debt. When you place your faith in Christ, your sin is forgiven. Your debt is canceled. You don't owe God and you don't owe you. While other faith systems give you something to do, Paul said it's all been done. God did what you could not do. Jesus took your sin and carried it away. Forgiveness is a gift God made available to everyone. But like any gift, it must be received.

Every faith tradition offers an answer to the question of what to do when we can't forgive ourselves. But only one person ever offered *himself* as the answer to that question.

Before we can begin to see the cross as something done for us, we have to see it as something done by us.

💬 John R. W. Scott

Jesus' words, "Forgive them for they do not know what they do," also apply to yourself.

💬 Eckhart Tolle

SECTION THREE:
QUESTIONS FOR REFLECTION

1 According to this section, what is required of you to receive God's forgiveness?

2 How do you feel about the idea that your sin has already been canceled?

3 What is standing in the way of you accepting God's forgiveness through Christ?

I think that if God forgives us we must forgive ourselves. Otherwise, it is almost like setting up ourselves as a higher tribunal than Him.

C. S. Lewis

BOTTOM LINES FOR CHAPTER 5

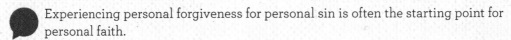 Experiencing personal forgiveness for personal sin is often the starting point for personal faith.

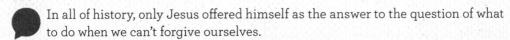 In all of history, only Jesus offered himself as the answer to the question of what to do when we can't forgive ourselves.

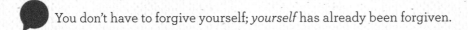 You don't have to forgive yourself; *yourself* has already been forgiven.

FOR THE NEXT GROUP MEETING:

Read and complete the questions for Chapter 6. Watch or listen to the Chapter 6 message at spmembers.com

At the next group meeting, we will examine grace. In everyday life, grace is radical, because we think life is all about getting what we deserve . . . good or bad. But grace is something different. It's about getting what we don't deserve. And it's key to the way we relate to God.

 Take advantage of essential chapter resources at:
spmembers.com

I am a most noteworthy sinner, but I have cried out to the Lord for grace and mercy, and they have covered me completely. I have found the sweetest consolation since I made it my whole purpose to enjoy His marvelous Presence.

● Christopher Columbus

GRACE

SECTION ONE:
SYSTEM FAILURE

We live in a world that rewards performance. It's ingrained in us from an early age. Answer the test questions right and you pass. Answer them wrong and you fail. Score the most points and you win. Score one point less than the competition and you lose. Do well in school and you'll get a good job. Do well at work and you'll get a promotion. Granted, it doesn't always work that way. But there's no denying that performance matters.

This performance orientation has the potential to shape our assumptions about God. When you ask people to describe what they think they have to do to *get on* or *stay on* God's good side, you get a list of behaviors—religious performance. Just about every aspect of life works that way. Why wouldn't it be the same with God? After all, if God created the world, shouldn't we assume he created the way the world operates? If that's the case, then isn't the cause-and-effect relationship between our performance and our value a reflection of some divine design?

While it would be easy to make that assumption, there are exceptions to the performance-valuation rule. A student fails an exam by two points, and the professor finds a way to give him a passing grade. A sales associate makes a less-than-stellar sales presentation, loses an account, and her manager responds by giving her another opportunity. A motorist is rear-ended and upon discovering the challenging circumstances of the careless driver, decides not to make an issue of it. Every once in a while, people get exactly what they don't deserve.

But even when we're the ones being let off the hook, we feel like something is wrong. It's great not to suffer consequences for what we've done, but it also feels like we've violated the system. Shouldn't people get what they deserve? Isn't that just?

Grace is the face that love wears when it meets imperfection.
● Joseph R. Cooke

It's not about my performance. It's about Jesus' performance for me. Grace isn't there for some future me but for the real me. The me who struggled. The me who was messy ... He loves me in my mess; he was not waiting until I cleaned myself up.

💬 Jefferson Bethke

88

SECTION ONE:
QUESTIONS FOR REFLECTION

1 Where do you feel the effects of a performance-based world most?

2 How does this influence your view of God?

3 When is a time that you have been let "off the hook"? How did you feel about it?

....

....

....

....

....

....

....

....

....

....

....

....

....

....

There is nothing we can do to make God love us more. There is nothing we can do to make God love us less.

● Philip Yancey

SECTION TWO:
UNDESERVED FAVOR

In Chapter 5, we discussed forgiveness. We discovered that Jesus' death paid for all our sins—past, present, and future. As the apostle Paul stated, through Christ, God

> . . . canceled the charge of our legal indebtedness, which stood against us. - Colossians 2:14

In other words, through Christ, God removed all the barriers to us being adopted into his family. Here is where the confusion often begins for many Christians. Having initiated a relationship with God by faith rather than by performance, their inclination is to manage their relationship with God according to the old system—the performance system. Before they know it, they're making assumptions about God's attitude toward them based on how well they perform. They attempt to earn what he's already given: favor. They quit thinking like family and begin performing like contracted labor. Old habits die hard.

Do you ever bargain with God? You know, "God, if you will [blank], I promise I will [blank]." Or, "God, if you will [blank], I will never [blank]." Think about that. Bargaining is based on two assumptions. First, someone has something the other party wants or needs. Second, the other party isn't about to do anybody any favors.

Do you believe you have earning potential with God? Do you believe you have something God wants or needs? Seems kind of silly when you stop to think about it. Don't feel bad. Most religious systems foster a bargaining mentality, and understandably so. That's how the world works. But remember, those who knew Jesus best made it remarkably clear . . . with God, grace is the rule, not the exception.

We're not the first generation of people to wrestle with this tension. The apostle Paul addressed this issue in several of his letters. To the Christians in the ancient city of

90

The dying Jesus is the evidence of God's anger toward sin; but the living Jesus is the proof of God's love and forgiveness.

● Lorenz Eifert

Colossae, he wrote:

> So then, just as you received Christ Jesus as Lord . . . - Colossians 2:6

That phrase alone deserves a comment. Based on our previous discussion, how does one receive Christ Jesus? *By faith*. What was it that compelled God to make salvation and forgiveness available to you in the first place? Grace. Undeserved favor. Nothing about *you* compelled him to. He just wanted to.

Paul continues:

> . . . So then, just as you received Christ Jesus as Lord, continue to live your lives in him. - Colossians 2:6

His point? Continue the way you started. Your relationship with God was initiated by faith in his gracious, undeserved offer of forgiveness. So, approach God every day from that same vantage point. Your life with Christ began in grace and it should continue in grace. Listen to how he concludes this passage:

> . . . rooted and built up in him, strengthened in the faith as you were taught, and overflowing with thankfulness. - Colossians 2:7

Did you notice what he said about bargaining? No? It's not there, is it? But look again at what he says about thankfulness. The Christian life is characterized by an overflow of thankfulness. You thank someone for what he's done. You bargain with someone for what you want him to do. God doesn't need anything *from* you, so you have no leverage with him. But he wants something *for* you, so you don't need any leverage.

In his letter to the Christians in Ephesus, Paul wrote:

> For it is by grace you have been saved, through faith—and this is not from yourselves, it is the gift of God—not by works, so that no one can boast. - Ephesians 2:8–9

You have been saved "by grace." God's forgiveness was, or hopefully soon will be, received as a gift. God does not view you through the filter of your performance. He views you through the filter of a father-to-child relationship. You didn't earn your way into God's good graces. You don't have to perform to stay there.

No matter how many good deeds we perform, they aren't the ticket to earning God's favor. God graces us in spite of what we do in this life, not because of.

● Bill Courtney

92

SECTION TWO:
QUESTIONS FOR REFLECTION

1 Is the idea of a relationship with God absent of performance a new idea to you? Explain.

2 How do bargaining-based Christianity and grace-based Christianity look different?

3 How would you explain the grace of God to someone else?

The gospel declares that no matter how dutiful or prayerful we are, we can't save ourselves. What Jesus did was sufficient.

Brennan Manning

SECTION THREE:
THE REASON FOR OBEDIENCE

Think back for a moment to a time when someone extended grace to you. Try to remember the most extreme case—an event where you received something so undeserved and unexpected you weren't even sure you could accept it. Have you ever been embarrassed by the gravity or significance of a gift or favor? If so, you can probably remember what you felt. If not, you can imagine what you would feel.

Now imagine if the person who bailed you out, forgave a loan, or gifted you unexpectedly said, "I don't want anything in return. This is a no-strings-attached gift. But if you feel the need to thank me, simply do for someone else to whatever degree you can what I've done for you." Chances are, you would look for an opportunity to do just that.

With that in mind, read how Jesus instructed his closest followers to live:

> "As I have loved you, so you must love one another." - John 13:34

Therein lies the basis and motivation for all the New Testament *"thou shalts"* and *"thou shalt nots."* We are to behave out of the overflow of our gratitude for how God through Christ behaved toward us. We don't obey to gain anything. We obey because of all we have already gained. For Jesus' followers, obedience is not a bargaining chip. It's a voluntary response of gratitude for what's already been given. Paul echoes that same sentiment when he writes:

> Get rid of all bitterness, rage and anger, brawling and slander, along with every form of malice. Be kind and compassionate to one another, forgiving each other, just as in Christ God forgave you. - Ephesians 4:31–32

These imperatives are not presented as means to an end. Paul didn't instruct his readers to be kind and compassionate so that God would be kind and compassionate back. He commanded them to embrace these virtues because God had already exhibited

The knowledge of God is very far from the love of Him.

💬 Blaise Pascal

those very things toward them. What comes next is even more extraordinary:

> Follow God's example, therefore, as dearly loved children and walk in the way of love, just as Christ loved us and gave himself up for us as a fragrant offering and sacrifice to God. - Ephesians 5:1–2

Again, no bargaining. No begging. We are to do for others what God in Christ has already done for us. One hundred percent of the "to dos" related to the Christian faith are a response to what God has "to done" for you. As the apostle John put it:

> We love because he first loved us. - 1 John 4:19

Grace is not a license to sin, but to walk in humility in the sight of God. Grace frees us to be active in the works of God. We are not tied up with how much we have done, or not done, but we learn by the grace of God to rest in His love.

● Curt McComis

95

96

SECTION THREE:
QUESTIONS FOR REFLECTION

1 What has characterized your exposure to or experience with Christians? Why do you think that is?

2 What should a Christian characterized by love and motivated by gratitude look like?

3 How would your life change if you viewed obedience to God's rules as opportunities to express gratitude?

To be grateful is to recognize the Love of God in everything He has given us—and He has given us everything . . . Gratitude, therefore, takes nothing for granted, is never unresponsive, is constantly awakening to new wonder . . .

● Thomas Merton

BOTTOM LINES FOR CHAPTER 6

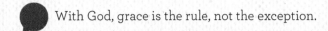 People often relate to God on a performance basis.

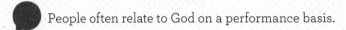 With God, grace is the rule, not the exception.

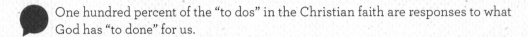 One hundred percent of the "to dos" in the Christian faith are responses to what God has "to done" for us.

FOR THE NEXT GROUP MEETING:

Read and complete the questions for Chapter 7. Watch or listen to the Chapter 7 message at spmembers.com

Starting Point is about exploring your faith. At the next group meeting, we'll talk about what faith is. Most people assume that having religious faith equates to holding certain beliefs about God. But it isn't quite that simple.

 Take advantage of essential chapter resources at:
spmembers.com

I do not at all understand the mystery of grace— only that it meets us where we are but does not leave us where it found us.

Anne Lamott

FAITH

SECTION ONE:
EVERYDAY FAITH

Faith is not a religious concept. It's a *human* concept. It's arguably the most powerful tool we have. The ability to believe something and act on it has launched everything from life-saving medical developments to genocide. Faith—or belief—fuels good and evil every day in every segment of the population. Everything that has been done, for good or bad, was done because somebody believed it could be and should be done. Every problem that has been solved was solved because somebody believed. Mountains have been moved by faith—medical mountains, scientific mountains, financial mountains.

Belief fuels anticipation and imagination. It enables us to picture a preferred future for us and the people around us. For all these reasons, and more, it is impossible to imagine life without faith.

Our ability to believe can work for us or against us. We all have a propensity to look for evidence to support what we already believe. It's easier for us to see that propensity in others, but we're all guilty. The problem is that when we adopt a belief that isn't true or isn't helpful, that propensity makes it difficult to change course. It can even cause us to actively resist what is true and helpful.

We're more open to data that substantiates what we already believe than information that conflicts with our viewpoints. Have you noticed how quickly you become defensive when information that contradicts your beliefs is presented? You may have experienced a bit of that during this study. Most participants do.

We are born believing. A man bears beliefs as a tree bears apples.
● Ralph Waldo Emerson

If you don't have solid beliefs, you cannot build a stable life. Beliefs are like the foundation of a building, and they are the foundation to build your life upon.

● Alfred A. Montapert

SECTION ONE:
QUESTIONS FOR REFLECTION

1 How is everyday faith, or belief, similar or dissimilar to religious faith?

2 How do your environment, family, and friends impact what you believe?

3 Have you ever changed what you believe? How did that happen?

Faith is taking the first step even when you don't see the whole staircase.

● Martin Luther King, Jr.

SECTION TWO:
BELIEF THAT VS. TRUST IN

Religious belief has the potential to become a self-fulfilling prophecy. Gather enough people who believe the same thing about anything and the next thing you know you have a movement. Or a new religion. Put a persuasive leader out front and the next thing you know, the world begins to change. This dynamic explains the rise of most popular religious movements. But it does not explain the rise of Christianity.

Throughout history, when leaders of popular movements died, their followers would band together to keep their messages and their missions alive. This was the case with the prophet Muhammad, who died of natural causes in AD 623. This was the case with Dr. Martin Luther King, Jr., who was assassinated for his beliefs in 1968. But when Jesus was crucified, the movement he began came to a screeching halt. The mission died with him because he *was* the mission. Jesus did not launch his movement around a new list of *believe thats*. At the center of his teaching was a single *believe in*. Jesus called upon his followers to believe in him. Not his ideas. *Him*. This theme is reflected in what is arguably the most popular statement in the

New Testament:

> For God so loved the world that he gave his one and only Son, that whoever *believes in him* shall not perish but have eternal life. - John 3:16

Toward the end of his life, it was evident to everyone that Jesus was claiming to be one with God. He even said as much.

> "I and the Father are one." - John 10:30
> "Anyone who has seen me has seen the Father." - John 14:9

Statements like these gave his enemies grounds to convict him of blasphemy. But many of Jesus' followers believed he was exactly who he claimed to be. When Jesus questioned his disciples regarding his identity, Peter blurted out,

> "You are the Messiah, the Son of the living God." - Matthew 16:16

Jesus' response?

> "Blessed are you, Simon son of Jonah, for this was not revealed to you by flesh and blood, but by my Father in heaven." - Matthew 16:17

Jesus allowed others to bestow upon him the title "Son of God." He did not resist

John the Baptist's description of him as "the Lamb of God who takes away the sin of the world!"[1] When his friend Lazarus died, Jesus announced to the dead man's sisters,

> "I am the resurrection and the life. The one who believes in me will live, even though they die." - John 11:25

Jesus didn't claim to know the truth about resurrection. He claimed to be *the* resurrection. He didn't ask Mary and Martha to believe a *that*. He asked them to trust *in* him.

From start to finish, the mission of Jesus was *Jesus*. He did not come to leave his followers with a collection of insights and parables to pass on to the next generation. He went too far for that to be the case. He claimed too much. So it should come as no surprise that when his disciples watched him die, they watched the movement die with him. Messiahs don't die. Sons of God can't be killed. It's impossible to crucify "the resurrection and the life." But there he was. Nailed to a Roman cross. And there he died.

When Jesus died, no one believed he was who he claimed to be.

When Jesus died, there were no Christians.

His followers fled. There was no discussion about how to keep his teaching alive. There was nothing to discuss. His life and his teaching were inseparable, and he was dead. His followers were left to choose between two explanations. Either he was confused or they had been duped. Yet, these were the very people who would later sacrifice their lives for their crucified leader.

This is where the story of Christianity parts ways with every other religious tradition and institution. This is where the story becomes both unexplainable and undeniable. It's unexplainable because there is no good explanation as to why Jesus' disciples later risked their lives to reengage. It's undeniable because here we are about two thousand years later discussing it. What's most important for our purposes is to understand that the hinge, the thing that made all the difference, was not something Jesus *taught*. It was something Jesus *did*.

He came back to life.[2]

Jesus rose from the dead and nobody was outside his tomb waiting. Not even his most loyal followers believed Jesus had come back to life until they saw him. And upon seeing him, they *believed*. They *trusted*. In a moment, they went from unbelief to belief.

Luke, who wrote both the gospel of Luke and the book of Acts, records what happened in Jerusalem when Jesus' followers went into the streets proclaiming his resurrection. Thousands gathered to hear the news. Peter was the appointed spokesman. His message was painfully direct. He didn't call to mind the teachings of Jesus. He didn't repeat his parables. Instead, he pointed into the crowd and summarized:

You killed him.
God raised him.
We've seen him.
Say you're sorry.[3]

Peter's willingness to stare down the very people who supported Jesus' trial and execution is impossible to explain apart from his own explanation. He had seen, touched, and conversed with his risen Messiah and Lord. With the resurrection of Jesus, there was a resurrection of faith.

1 John 1:29

2 Luke 24:6
3 Acts 2-3

108

SECTION TWO:
QUESTIONS FOR REFLECTION

1 How do Jesus' statements about himself make him unique? What do they tell us about him?

2 Why was Jesus' death particularly devastating for the continuation of his message?

3 How does the disciples' behavior lend credibility to the claims of Christianity?

....

....

....

....

....

....

....

....

....

....

....

....

....

Jesus does not give recipes that show the way to God as other teachers of religion do. He is himself the way.

● Karl Barth

SECTION THREE:
FAITH ISN'T BLIND

Following Jesus requires faith. Specifically, it requires one to place his or her trust in Jesus. Not the teachings of Jesus—the person of Jesus. Christianity does not require blind faith. Christianity is an informed faith. At the center is an event attested to by eyewitnesses who, by their own accounts, lost faith when Jesus died, but regained it when he rose from the dead. The foundation of Christianity is not a list of *believe thats*. It is a single *trust in*.

Christians don't believe Jesus rose from the dead because the Bible says so. Christians believe Jesus rose from the dead because Matthew and John, eyewitnesses, said so. Christians believe because Luke, a first-century doctor, claimed to have thoroughly investigated the events surrounding the life and crucifixion of Jesus and concluded that Jesus rose from the dead. Luke spent the second half of his life traveling throughout the Roman Empire telling that story. We believe Jesus rose from the dead because Peter believed he did. Peter, who on the night of Jesus' arrest denied knowing him, became the leader of the church in Jerusalem, the city where these events took place. Christians believe Jesus rose from the dead because James, the brother of Jesus, claims it was true. James trusted in his brother as his Savior.

Christians believe because Mark, a friend and companion of Peter, testified to the truth of Jesus' resurrection. Last, and by his own account least, Christians believe because the apostle Paul believed. Paul, who stepped into history as a persecutor of Christians, came to believe Jesus was the Son of God and that he physically rose from the dead.

These witnesses paid a high price for their faith. Most were martyred. Throughout history, courageous men and women have given their lives for what they believed. This group was different. They gave up their lives for what they said they saw—*the resurrected Jesus.*

Like every religion, Christianity requires faith. Specifically, Christianity requires faith in a person. This is why for anyone investigating Christianity, the first question that must be answered is, *Who is Jesus?*

Faith is not intelligent understanding; faith is deliberate commitment to a Person where I see no way.

● Oswald Chambers

112

SECTION THREE:
QUESTIONS FOR REFLECTION

1 Is there any belief or cause you are willing to die for?

2 How central is the resurrection to the validity of the Christian message?

3 How has your view of Jesus been impacted over the past seven weeks?

Be sure you put your feet in the right place; then stand firm.

Abraham Lincoln

BOTTOM LINES FOR CHAPTER 7

 Faith is one of the most powerful tools at humanity's disposal.

 The thing that makes Jesus different from other religious leaders isn't something he taught; it's something he did. He died and came back to life.

 Christianity requires faith in a person. This is why for anyone investigating Christianity, the first question that must be answered is, *Who is Jesus?*

FOR THE NEXT GROUP MEETING:

Read and complete the questions for Chapter 8. Watch or listen to the Chapter 8 message at spmembers.com

The next meeting will be your last one for this study. Over the past seven meetings, you've explored faith and met some new people who may have challenged you in new ways. Take some time to reflect on your Starting Point experience.

 Take advantage of essential chapter resources at:
spmembers.com

Faith isn't the ability to believe long and far into the misty future. It's simply taking God at His Word and taking the next step.

Joni Eareckson Tada

INVITATION

SECTION ONE:
NEW PURPOSE

Odds are, you want your life to matter. Christians believe this desire is the thumbprint of God on our souls ... that thing in us that looks beyond ourselves and wonders *why . . . why are we here . . . why does anything exist?* That is a uniquely human characteristic. The notion that life is supposed to be meaningful drives us to look for meaning. It's as if we know intuitively that our individual selves are not enough. We sense that this thirst we have will never be quenched until we connect with something greater than ourselves. Eventually we realize that our individual glory isn't enough. There's no satisfaction there.

C. S. Lewis hinted at this idea when he wrote:

> If I find in myself desires which nothing in this world can satisfy, the only logical explanation is that I was made for another world. —*Mere Christianity*

The yearning for purpose is not a uniquely Christian experience. It is part of the human condition. But for most, it leads to frustration and disillusionment. When we're young, we dream of changing the world. But as we get older, it seems the world changes us. We are tempted to lower our standards and adjust our expectations. If we aren't careful, we grow cynical and critical.

What if God has a plan for you that is not contingent upon what you've done or even who you've been until now? What if restarting your faith is actually an opportunity to restart your life? Jesus said something to that effect. He said part of the reason he came was so that we could have *life*.[1] About twenty years later, Paul would remind Timothy that those who follow Jesus would "take hold of the life that is truly life."[2]

That thing in you that hopes your short time on this planet has significance beyond your time on this planet is a yearning to connect with God's plan for you. He's given you the raw materials. Talent. Opportunity. Under the canopy of his grace and mercy, those otherwise random traits and quirks take on significance. Your uniqueness positions you to play a special role in a grand story that is constantly unfolding around you. God wants you to discover the full expression of who you are. But you can't do that by yourself. Your uniqueness finds its fullest and best expression when connected to his divine purpose in the world.

1 John 10:10
2 1 Timothy 6:19

The space where someone's need and your gifts meet is the space for service, an opportunity, and perhaps a calling.

💬 Dr. Henry Cloud

120

SECTION ONE:
QUESTIONS FOR REFLECTION

1 When have you felt the need for deeper meaning in your life?

2 What do you see as your gifts and talents?

3 What do you think of the idea that God has a plan for your life?

**Because God has made us for Himself, our hearts
are restless until they rest in Him.**

💬 St. Augustine

SECTION TWO:
EKKLESIA

In the last chapter we read about a conversation Jesus had with his disciples. He asked what the word on the street was concerning his identity. Did people think he was just another rabbi, a teacher, perhaps a zealot? After hearing a variety of answers, he stopped and asked,

"But what about you?" he asked.

"Who do you say I am?"

Simon Peter answered, "You are the Messiah, the Son of the living God."
– Matthew 16:15–16

What Jesus said next is of extreme importance. If he believed Peter was caught up in the crowd-induced hysteria surrounding his miracles and teaching, this would have been the perfect time to set the record straight. After all, he had introduced the topic. But he didn't caution Peter; he encouraged him:

Jesus replied, "Blessed are you, Simon son of Jonah, for this was not revealed to you by flesh and blood, but by my Father in heaven."
- Matthew 16:17

Think about that. Jesus not only affirmed Peter's rather extreme estimation, he went so far as to accredit his answer to God! This was the equivalent of saying, "Peter, not only do I agree with you; God agrees as well." But Jesus wasn't finished.

"And I tell you that you are Peter, and on this rock I will build my church, and the gates of Hades will not overcome it." - Matthew 16:18

Using a play on words, Jesus affirms Peter's statement while revealing his vision for the future. Just like "Peter" means "rock," Peter's answer to Jesus' question would be the bedrock confession of a new community of like-minded people—*the church*.

The word *church* in this passage is translated from the Greek word *ekklesia*. To the original audience, this was not a religious term. It simply described a gathering or assembly

The *True Church* can never fail. For it is based upon a rock.
● T. S. Eliot

122

of people called out for a specific purpose. Any type of assembly—civic, military, or otherwise—could be described as an *ekklesia*. Standing outside a city named for both a Greek king and a Roman emperor, Jesus announced his plans to institute a new gathering, a unique assembly of people. The common ground of this new movement would not be a national, social, or political agenda. It would be him. It would be a gathering of people who believed that he was exactly who Peter declared him to be—*the Messiah, the Son of the living God.*

Jesus' declaration must have sounded odd (perhaps even a bit grandiose) to his disciples. After all, it was just the twelve of them plus Jesus. But Jesus did exactly what he promised to do. The fact that about two thousand years later you are participating in a conversation about Jesus is proof that Jesus was true to his word. Jesus' reference to *Hades* was a reference to death. His point was unmistakable to his original audience. Death—not even *his* death—would stop the *ekklesia* of Jesus.

As we discovered in the previous chapter, Jesus' death and subsequent resurrection empowered his followers to take his gospel into the streets of Jerusalem. There, in the very city where he was tried and crucified, the church was born. There were no buildings. No creeds. No Bible as we have it today. The church was a growing gathering of men and women who had one thing in common. They believed Jesus was the Son of God.

I am blown away that my God, who could do this all by Himself, would choose to let me be a little part of it.

● Katie J. Davis

123

124

SECTION TWO:
QUESTIONS FOR REFLECTION

1 What do you associate with the word *church*?

2 Do you feel like the church has drifted from what Jesus originally intended? If so, how?

3 What would your response be if Jesus were to ask you, "Who do you say I am?"

....

....

....

....

....

....

....

....

....

....

....

....

....

The operation of the Church is entirely set up for the sinner; which creates much misunderstanding among the smug.
Flannery O'Connor

SECTION THREE:
YOUR NEXT STEP

Jesus did not predict a religion. He did not predict an institution. He predicted a people. He anticipated an assembly of imperfect people whose faith in a resurrected Savior would move them to embrace a lifestyle that reflected the grace, forgiveness, and kindness of their heavenly Father. For many, however, *grace*, *forgiveness*, and *kindness* are not terms they would use to describe the local church. You may count yourself among that group. A bad church experience may have driven you away from faith. The good news is that in every generation there is a contingency of believers that refuses to view church as a place. There have always been, and will always be, Jesus followers who view the church as a movement—a movement characterized by love for one another and for the world.

No doubt you are grateful if someone invited you into this conversation. At some point, you probably felt a wave of gratitude for your group leaders. You may have wondered, *Who are all these people and where do they find the motivation and energy to do all of this?* What you've experienced and observed these past several weeks *is* the church. Your life has been enriched by people you don't even know doing what they are gifted to do because someone did the same for them.

As you start or restart your faith, our hope is that discussing your questions will be a first step, not a final step. Our prayer is that your newfound or refound faith will instill in you a desire to help others rediscover their faith. In short, we hope you will take an active role in your generation's Jesus gathering.

So, take your place in the story by finding your place in the local church. This is your opportunity to do for others what others have done for you.

A life not lived for others is not a life.
Mother Teresa

I used to think you had to be special for God to use you, but now I know you simply need to say yes.

💬 Bob Goff

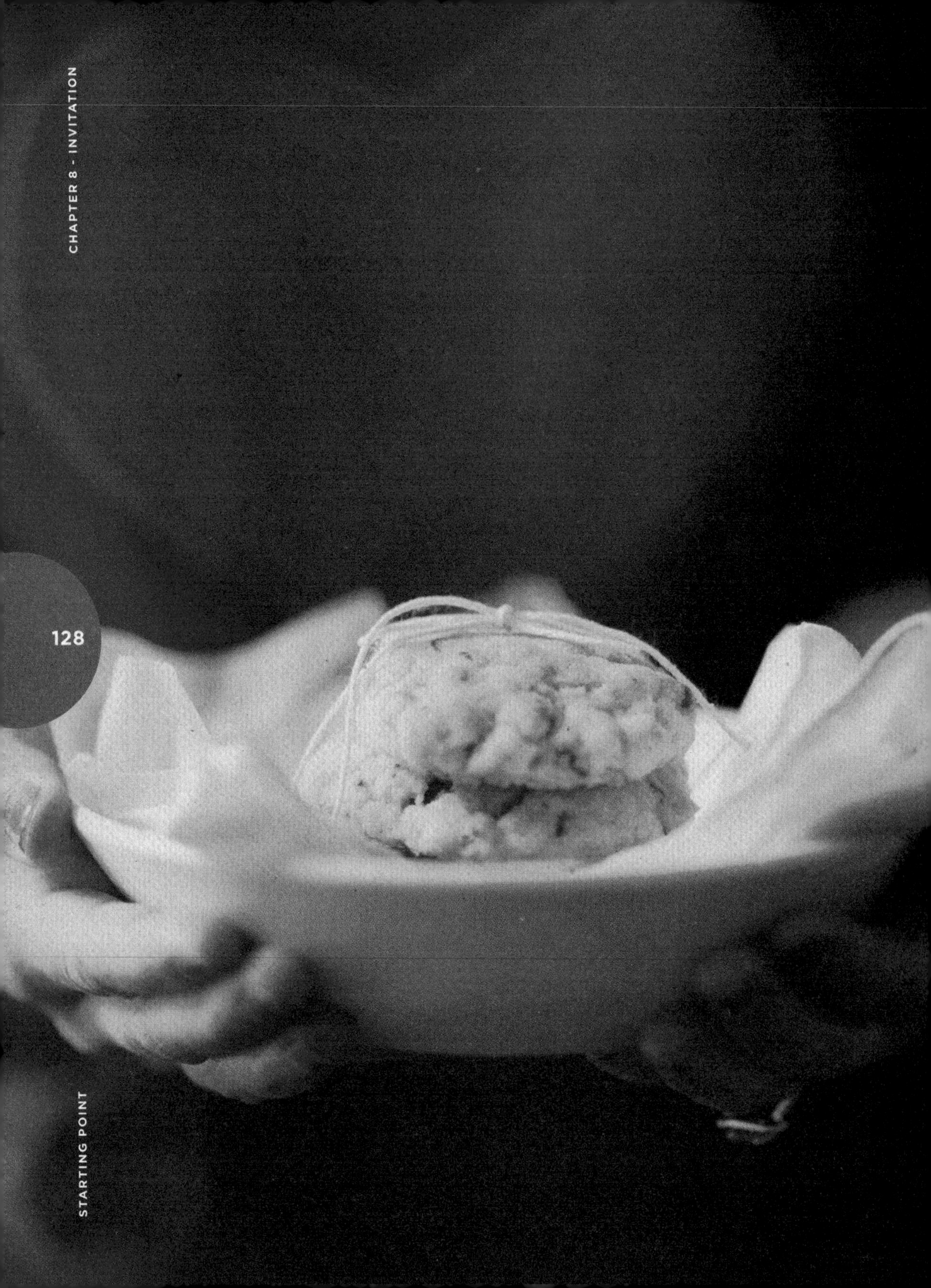

SECTION THREE:
QUESTIONS FOR REFLECTION

1 Where could you see your gifts and passions being used in the church?

2 What will you take away from this Starting Point group experience?

3 What feels like the very next step for you in your faith journey?

Since God knows our future, our personalities, and our capacity to listen, He isn't ever going to say more to us than we can deal with at the moment.

● Charles Stanley

BOTTOM LINES FOR CHAPTER 8

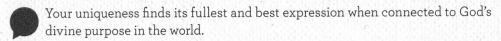 Your uniqueness finds its fullest and best expression when connected to God's divine purpose in the world.

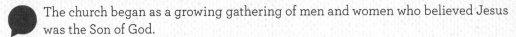 The church began as a growing gathering of men and women who believed Jesus was the Son of God.

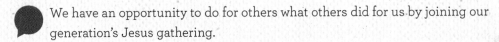 We have an opportunity to do for others what others did for us by joining our generation's Jesus gathering.

AFTER YOUR GROUP ENDS:

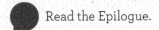 Read the Epilogue.

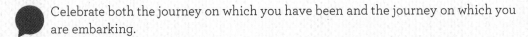 Celebrate both the journey on which you have been and the journey on which you are embarking.

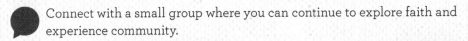 Connect with a small group where you can continue to explore faith and experience community.

 Take advantage of essential chapter resources at:
spmembers.com

I think that's the true litmus test for someone who has become closer to Jesus: their heart is more loving, accepting, childlike, less believing that they have all the answers and more believing in Him.

● Donald Miller

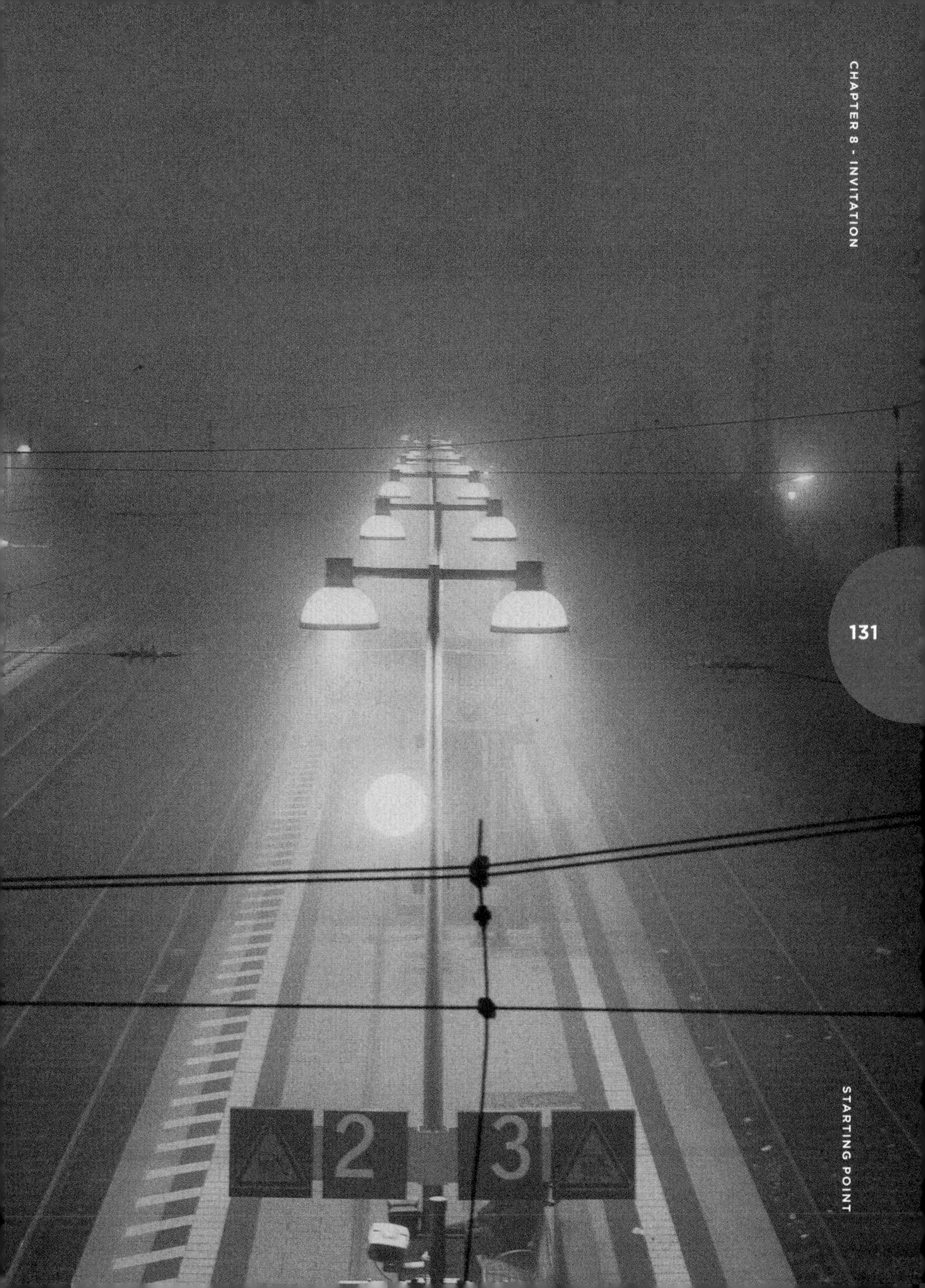
2
3

APPENDIX

APPENDIX:
WHAT'S YOUR STORY?

The idea of telling your personal story to the other members of your Starting Point group may make you a little uncomfortable, but it doesn't have to be a big production. The goal isn't to be comprehensive. It's to give the other people in your group a sense of what makes you uniquely you.

What parts of your story should you tell?

If you really think about your story, it's probably centered around people, places, and events. Those three categories capture how we interact with the world around us.

One way to organize your thoughts about your personal story is to use the space provided to identify people who have played significant roles in your life, places that are special to you, and events that have affected you. It's as simple as that.

You probably can't talk about all the people, places, and events referenced above since you will only have five to ten minutes to share. But this will give you a good start. From here, you can think through the parts of your story that are the most important

to emphasize. It's your story. You are free to share what you want to share.

Above all, remember this. You may think the other members of your group aren't interested in your story, but that's not true. Most of us are curious about the people around us. And we're predisposed to empathize and connect with others. Your story will help draw the other members of your group closer. You will be amazed how many people will relate to parts of your story.

Stories are the creative conversion of life itself into a more powerful, clearer, more meaningful experience. They are the currency of human contact.
● Robert McKee

KEY PEOPLE:

....

....

....

....

....

KEY PLACES:

....

....

....

....

....

KEY EVENTS:

....

....

....

....

....

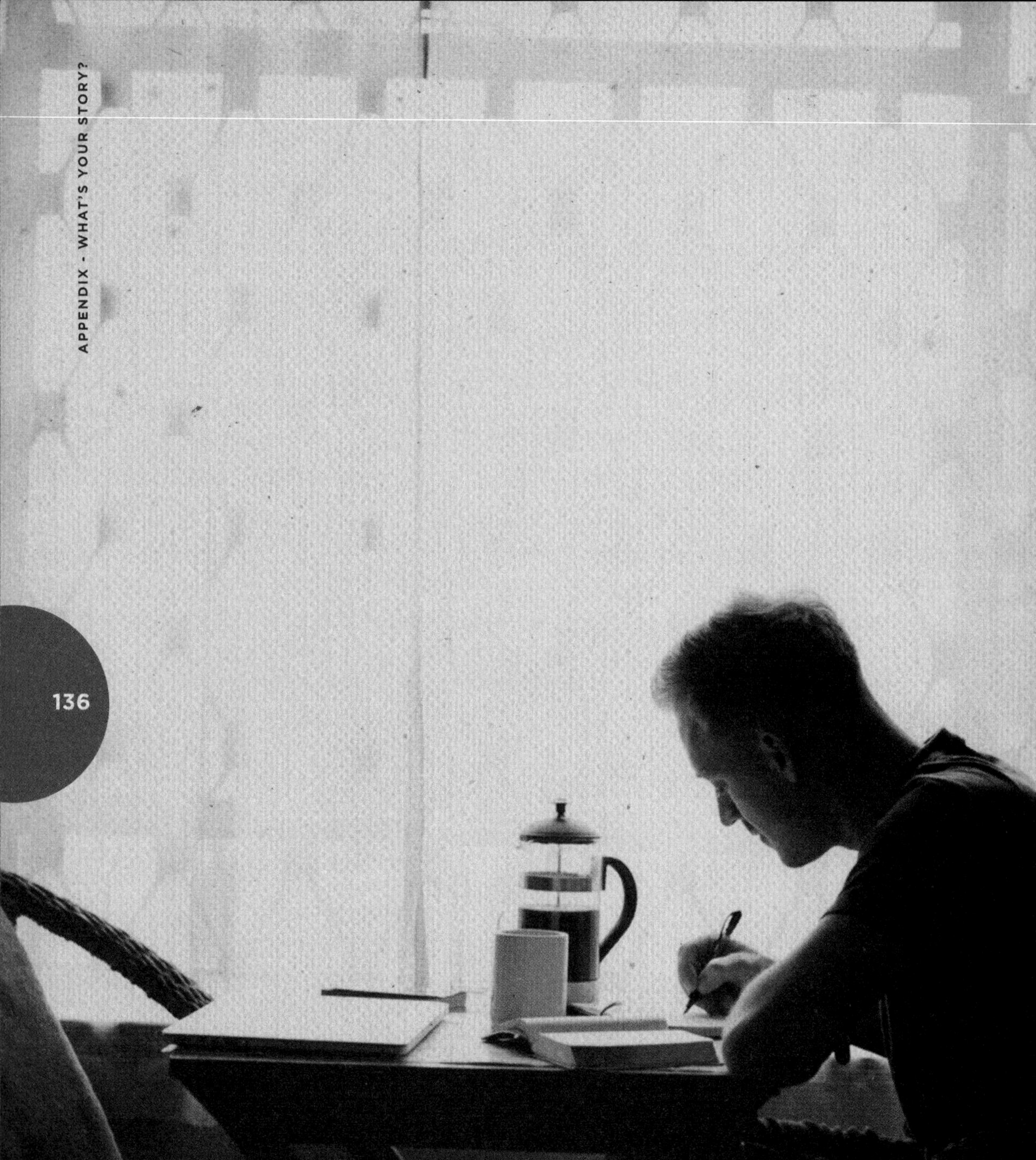

NOTES FOR YOUR STORY

Be yourself; everyone else is already taken.
💬 Oscar Wilde

APPENDIX:
BIBLE READING GUIDE

If you're interested in reading the Bible, you don't have to start at the beginning and read to the very end. In fact, that's probably not the best way to get started. So, we've put together a few options that make reading the Bible enjoyable and helpful. Whichever option you choose, it's a good idea to ask yourself the following questions as you read. These questions will help you better understand what you're reading and how it applies to your life:

1. What does the passage say?

2. What does it mean?

3. How does it apply to my life?

EXPLORING JESUS IN 21 DAYS

The Gospels—Matthew, Mark, Luke, John—are four different accounts of Jesus' life. This reading plan explores two of them: Luke and John.

Day 1: Luke 1–2
Day 2: Luke 3–4
Day 3: Luke 5–6
Day 4: Luke 7–8
Day 5: Luke 9–10
Day 6: Luke 11–12
Day 7: Luke 13–15
Day 8: Luke 16–18
Day 9: Luke 19–20
Day 10: Luke 21–22
Day 11: Luke 23–24

Day 12: John 1–2
Day 13: John 3–4
Day 14: John 5–6
Day 15: John 7–8
Day 16: John 9–10
Day 17: John 11–12
Day 18: John 13–15
Day 19: John 16–17
Day 20: John 18–19
Day 21: John 20–21

SAMPLING SCRIPTURE IN TEN WEEKS

This reading plan includes entire books or significant portions of books spanning different time periods and literary genres in the biblical story. As you read this plan, you'll experience historical narrative, songs, prophetic messages, travel accounts, and personal letters. You'll also read the well-known stories of creation, the exodus, and the early Christian movement. You'll meet biblical figures such as King David, the prophet Jonah, and Jesus. The purpose of this reading plan is to expose you to the grand redemptive storyline of the Bible.

Week 1: Genesis 1–25
Week 2: Exodus 1–20; Ruth
Week 3: 1 Samuel 16–31, 2 Samuel 1–7
Week 4: Psalms 1–41
Week 5: Amos, Obadiah, Jonah, Micah
Week 6: Esther, Ezra
Week 7: Mark
Week 8: Acts 1–12, 1 Peter
Week 9: Acts 13–28
Week 10: Romans, Ephesians

140

READING THE BIBLE IN ONE YEAR

If you follow this plan, you'll read through the entire Bible in a year. Readings are divided by weeks instead of days in order to give you some flexibility. The plan begins in the Old Testament and moves in chronological order through the end of the New Testament. This means you'll do a fair amount of hopping around from week to week since the books of the Bible are not ordered chronologically.

Week 1: Genesis 1–25

Week 2: Genesis 26–50

Week 3: Job 1–24

Week 4: Job 25–42, Exodus 1–10

Week 5: Exodus 11–34

Week 6: Exodus 35–40, Leviticus 1–15

Week 7: Leviticus 16–27, Numbers 1–4

Week 8: Numbers 5–21

Week 9: Numbers 22–36, Psalms 1–17

Week 10: Psalms 18–55

Week 11: Psalms 56–94

Week 12: Psalms 95–150

Week 13: Deuteronomy 1–19

Week 14: Deuteronomy 20–34, Proverbs 1–7

Week 15: Proverbs 8–31

Week 16: Ecclesiastes, Joshua 1–10

Week 17: Joshua 11–24, Judges 1–5

Week 18: Judges 6–21, Ruth

Week 19: Song of Songs, 1 Samuel 1–16

Week 20: 1 Samuel 17–31, 2 Samuel 1–7

Week 21: 2 Samuel 8–24

Week 22: 1 Kings 1–18

Week 23: 1 Kings 19–22, 2 Kings 1–16

Week 24: 2 Kings 17–25, Isaiah 1–11

Week 25: Isaiah 12–37

Week 26: Isaiah 38–59

Week 27: Isaiah 60–66, Jeremiah 1–14

Week 28: Jeremiah 15–36

Week 29: Jeremiah 37–52

Week 30: Lamentations, 1 Chronicles 1–12

Week 31: 1 Chronicles 13–29, 2 Chronicles 1–7

Week 32: 2 Chronicles 8–38

Week 33: Ezekiel 1–20

Week 34: Ezekiel 21–38

Week 35: Ezekiel 39–48, Daniel

Week 36: Hosea, Joel, Amos

Week 37: Ezra, Nehemiah

Week 38: Esther, Obadiah, Jonah, Micah

Week 39: Nahum, Habakkuk, Zephaniah, Haggai, Zechariah, Malachi

Week 40: Matthew 1–17

Week 41: Matthew 18–28, Hebrews 1–8

Week 42: Hebrews 9–13, James, Mark 1–9

Week 43: Mark 10–16, 1 Peter, 2 Peter, Jude

Week 44: Luke 1–15

Week 45: Luke 16–24, Acts 1–7

Week 46: Acts 8–21

Week 47: Acts 22–28, Romans

Week 48: 1 Corinthians, 2 Corinthians

Week 49: Galatians, Ephesians, Philippians, Colossians, 1 and 2 Thessalonians

Week 50: 1 and 2 Timothy, Titus, Philemon, John 1–10

Week 51: John 11–21; 1, 2, and 3 John

Week 52: Revelation

EPILOGUE

We've come to the end of the beginning. You've begun a dynamic conversation that we hope will last a lifetime—a conversation that connects you with God and with others. We designed Starting Point to be a safe place to ask questions about God and faith. Just because your group has ended doesn't mean all of your questions have been answered. In fact, as you continue to investigate and experience God, more questions will surface. That's okay.

We hope you'll not only be comfortable searching for the answers yourself, but that you will continue to seek a deeper relationship with God and healthy relationships with those on the same journey. Through your Starting Point conversations, you've learned more about God, others, and yourself. We encourage you to continue conversations about faith through a community setting.

We've talked about a lot of important things. One of the most important is who Jesus is and what he did for you. You may or may not be ready to put your faith in Jesus Christ. Wherever you are on your faith journey, we pray you will continue it. God loves *you*. God desires a growing relationship with *you*. He's reaching toward *you*. What is your next step in this journey?